ENDANGERED AND THREATENED ANIMALS

THE CHEETAH

A MyReportLinks.com Book

BLOOMINGTON, ILLINOIS
PUBLIC LIBRARY

Lisa Harkrader

MyReportLinks.com Books

an imprint of

Enslow Publishers, Inc.

Box 398, 40 Industrial Road
Berkeley Heights, NJ 07922
USA

MyReportLinks.com Books, an imprint of Enslow Publishers, Inc. MyReportLinks® is a registered trademark of Enslow Publishers, Inc.

Library of Congress Cataloging-in-Publication Data

Harkrader, Lisa.
  The cheetah / Lisa Harkrader.
     p. cm. — (Endangered and threatened animals)
  Includes bibliographical references and index.
  ISBN 0-7660-5065-3
  1. Cheetah—Juvenile literature. 2. Endangered species—Juvenile literature. I. Title. II. Series.
  QL737.C23H356 2005
  599.75'9—dc22
                              2004009824

Printed in the United States of America

10 9 8 7 6 5 4 3 2 1

To Our Readers:
Through the purchase of this book, you and your library gain access to the Report Links that specifically back up this book.
The Publisher will provide access to the Report Links that back up this book and will keep these Report Links up to date on **www.myreportlinks.com** for five years from the book's first publication date.
We have done our best to make sure all Internet addresses in this book were active and appropriate when we went to press. However, the author and the Publisher have no control over, and assume no liability for, the material available on those Internet sites or on other Web sites they may link to.
The usage of the MyReportLinks.com Books Web site is subject to the terms and conditions stated on the Usage Policy Statement on **www.myreportlinks.com**.
A password may be required to access the Report Links that back up this book. The password is found on the bottom of page 4 of this book.
Any comments or suggestions can be sent by e-mail to comments@myreportlinks.com or to the address on the back cover.

Contents

Report Links 4

Cheetah Facts 10

1   The Endangered Cheetah 11

2   The Fastest Animal on Land 19

3   Life as a Cheetah 26

4   Threats to Cheetahs 32

5   Saving the Cheetah 37

    The Endangered and
    Threatened Wildlife List 45

    Chapter Notes 46

    Further Reading 47

    Index 48

MyReportLinks.com Books
Great Books, Great Links, Great for Research!

The Internet sites listed on the next five pages can save you hours of research time. These Internet sites—we call them "Report Links"—are constantly changing, but we keep them up to date on our Web site.

Give it a try! Type http://www.myreportlinks.com into your browser, click on the series title, then the book title, and scroll down to the Report Links listed for this book.

The Report Links will bring you to great source documents, photographs, and illustrations. MyReportLinks.com Books save you time, feature Report Links that are kept up to date, and make report writing easier than ever!

Please see "To Our Readers" on the copyright page for important information about this book, the MyReportLinks.com Web site, and the Report Links that back up this book.

Please enter **ECH1816** if asked for a password.

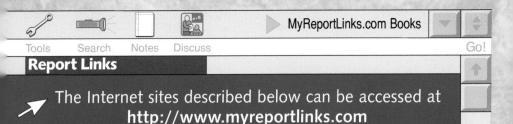
The Internet sites described below can be accessed at
http://www.myreportlinks.com

*EDITOR'S CHOICE

▶**Cheetah**
Learn about cheetahs from this San Diego Zoo Web site. Information on
this species includes physical characteristics, life span, conservation status,
and more.

Link to this Internet site from http://www.myreportlinks.com

*EDITOR'S CHOICE

▶**Cheetahs in a Hot Spot**
This PBS site provides a look at the world's fastest land animal—the cheetah.
Learn what makes the cheetah such a deadly hunter.

Link to this Internet site from http://www.myreportlinks.com

*EDITOR'S CHOICE

▶**Cheetah Conservation Fund (CCF)**
The Cheetah Conservation Fund (CCF) is an internationally recognized
organization that conducts research and provides educational outreach
programs on cheetahs and their ecosystems. Learn more about this
organization and cheetahs from their Web site.

Link to this Internet site from http://www.myreportlinks.com

*EDITOR'S CHOICE

▶**Meet the Cheetahs**
Scientists from the Wildlife Conservation Society have been tracking—
and naming—individual cheetahs in Tanzania's Serengeti National Park
since 1975. At this site, read a brief biography and view pictures of
each animal.

Link to this Internet site from http://www.myreportlinks.com

*EDITOR'S CHOICE

▶**Cheetah—*Acinonyx jubatus***
Cheetahs are the oldest cats on earth, appearing long before lions and
tigers. This Web site offers a history of this amazing cat species.

Link to this Internet site from http://www.myreportlinks.com

*EDITOR'S CHOICE

▶**International Society for Endangered Cats**
This Web site from the International Society for Endangered Cats offers
fact sheets on the thirty-seven species of cats, broken down by continent.
Read about the organization and the work it does to help conserve the
world's wild cat populations.

Link to this Internet site from http://www.myreportlinks.com

The Internet sites described below can be accessed at
http://www.myreportlinks.com

African Wildlife Foundation: Wildlives: Cheetah
The African Wildlife Foundation is dedicated to the survival of local wildlife
and habitats and especially endangered animals. This page describes efforts to
save Africa's cheetah population.

Link to this Internet site from http://www.myreportlinks.com

AfriCat
The AfriCat Foundation, based in Namibia, Africa, works to conserve large
carnivore species, including cheetahs, leopards, and lions. Learn more about
their efforts from their Web site.

Link to this Internet site from http://www.myreportlinks.com

Chance the Cheetah Fights for Future in Baghdad
After the war began in Iraq, most of the animals in the Baghdad Zoo were
poached for food, sold, or kept as pets. Two cheetahs were saved from terrible
conditions and were named Chance and Lucky. Learn about their story from
this article.

Link to this Internet site from http://www.myreportlinks.com

Cheetah, *Acinonyx jubatus*
Cheetahs were first brought to a North American zoo in 1871. This site offers
a history of cheetahs in zoos as well as an overview of the big cat.

Link to this Internet site from http://www.myreportlinks.com

Cheetah Census Seeks to Map and Halt the Cat's Rapid Decline
The De Wildt Cheetah and Wildlife Trust near Johannesburg, South Africa,
has launched a countrywide census to count South Africa's cheetahs.
This article from the Environmental News Network Web site talks about
the project.

Link to this Internet site from http://www.myreportlinks.com

Cheetah Conservation Botswana
Coexisting with cheetahs is something that conservationists want farmers
in Botswana to do. At this site, read more about cheetah management and
predator control and watch a video about the organization and its work.

Link to this Internet site from http://www.myreportlinks.com

Report Links

The Internet sites described below can be accessed at
http://www.myreportlinks.com

▶ **Cheetah Conservation in Southern Africa**
This Web site talks about the cheetah, why it is endangered, and what is
being done to help protect the world's population of cheetahs.

Link to this Internet site from http://www.myreportlinks.com

▶ **Cheetah Conservation Station**
At the Web site for the Smithsonian National Zoological Park (better
known as the National Zoo), learn about the zoo's Cheetah Conservation
Center. Meet the National Zoo's cheetahs, and get information and images
of these cats.

Link to this Internet site from http://www.myreportlinks.com

▶ **Cheetah Outreach**
Based in South Africa, Cheetah Outreach works to ensure the survival
of cheetahs by increasing awareness of endangerment, breeding the cats
in captivity, and other methods. At the Cheetah Outreach site, read about
this organization's efforts and successes.

Link to this Internet site from http://www.myreportlinks.com

▶ **The Cheetah Spot**
Did you know that cheetahs are primarily diurnal, meaning they hunt in
the cool morning and early evening? Did you know they sometimes chirp,
sounding more like birds than cats? This site offers interesting information
about cheetahs.

Link to this Internet site from http://www.myreportlinks.com

▶ **The Cheetah's Race for Survival**
This article focuses on the fight to save cheetahs in Namibia through
the use of Anatolian shepherds, or Kangal dogs. These dogs are bred
to protect livestock from cheetah attacks, making farmers less likely
to kill cheetahs.

Link to this Internet site from http://www.myreportlinks.com

▶ **Cheetahs: Ghosts of the Grasslands**
On this site from *National Geographic*, view images of cheetahs in
Tanzania. Click on photos to enlarge them for an even better look.

Link to this Internet site from http://www.myreportlinks.com

The Internet sites described below can be accessed at
http://www.myreportlinks.com

▶ **Conservation of Asiatic Cheetah Project (CACP)**
Educating the community and reducing the number of annual gun licenses
are two critical steps toward ensuring the survival of the cheetah in Iran.
At this site, learn more about the efforts to save the Asiatic cheetah.

Link to this Internet site from http://www.myreportlinks.com

▶ **De Wildt Cheetah and Wildlife Centre**
Cheetahs do not breed very well in captivity, making it difficult to help their
numbers grow. The De Wildt Cheetah and Wildlife Centre has made great
strides in captive breeding with nearly six hundred cheetah cubs bred since
1971. Learn more about the center's work from its Web site.

Link to this Internet site from http://www.myreportlinks.com

▶ **Educating Cheetah**
This article from the National Wildlife Federation discusses the role of
the mother cheetah in teaching her cheetah cubs how to hunt and fend
for themselves.

Link to this Internet site from http://www.myreportlinks.com

▶ **Endangered Species Information, U.S. Fish & Wildlife Service**
The United States Fish and Wildlife Service lists threatened and endangered
animals and plants worldwide. This USFWS page offers links to the database
in which those species, including the cheetah, are listed.

Link to this Internet site from http://www.myreportlinks.com

▶ **Fierce Dogs Protect Livestock, Cheetahs in Africa**
Anatolian shepherds are dogs that are being used to guard livestock on
Namibian farms and ranches, and in the process are helping save the local
cheetah population. This *National Geographic* article discusses the program
in more detail.

Link to this Internet site from http://www.myreportlinks.com

▶ **Honolulu Zoo: Cheetah**
Cheetahs have an interesting history, one that started about 5 million years
ago. Since cheetahs are endangered, that history may soon come to an end.
At this zoo Web site, read more about the cheetah's plight and take a quiz.

Link to this Internet site from http://www.myreportlinks.com

The Internet sites described below can be accessed at
http://www.myreportlinks.com

▶**How Much Do Animals Sleep?**
The chart on this Web site displays three pieces of information: species name, average total sleep time (percent of twenty-four hours), and average total sleep time (hours/day). Learn how long cheetahs and other animals usually sleep.

Link to this Internet site from http://www.myreportlinks.com

▶**Lincoln Park Zoo: Cheetahs**
The Web site from Chicago's Lincoln Park Zoo includes an informative page about cheetahs. The zoo also conducts research on better ways to breed cheetahs in captivity.

Link to this Internet site from http://www.myreportlinks.com

▶**Namibia**
Namibia, a country in southwestern Africa, is home to the largest population of wild cheetahs. Learn some basic facts about the country to better understand the cheetah. Follow the "Exploring Namibia" link for more information.

Link to this Internet site from http://www.myreportlinks.com

▶**Reproductive Technologies and Conservation of Endangered Cats**
Twenty-three of the thirty-seven cat species (or their subspecies) are endangered. This Web site from the National Zoo talks about the latest technologies that scientists are using to breed these cats.

Link to this Internet site from http://www.myreportlinks.com

▶**Species Survival Commission—The Cat Specialist Group**
The Cat Specialist Group of the Species Survival Commission, part of the IUCN–World Conservation Union, provides data on wild cats, advises governments on conservation strategies, and helps develop conservation projects. At this site, read more about the group's work.

Link to this Internet site from http://www.myreportlinks.com

▶**ZSL Living Conservation**
This Web site from the Zoological Society of London describes the Serengeti Cheetah Project, which has tracked individual cheetahs on Tanzania's Serengeti plains for nearly fifteen years.

Link to this Internet site from http://www.myreportlinks.com

Scientific Name

Acinonyx jubatus

Range

Central and southern Africa and a remote mountain region in northwestern Iran. The largest population of wild cheetahs lives in the southern African country of Namibia.

Average Length

4.5 feet (1.5 meters); their tails add another 30 inches (75 centimeters).

Average Weight

80 to 140 pounds (36 to 64 kilograms)

Fur

Tawny fur with black spots over the entire body except the throat and stomach, which are white

Maximum Speed

70 miles per hour (112 kilometers per hour) in sprints of less than one minute

Habitat

Savannas, which are grassy plains, and woodlands

Breeding Season

No particular season

Gestation Period

90 days

Number in a Litter

1 to 8 cubs; 3 to 5 is average.

Life Span

Less than 10 years in the wild; 15 years or longer in captivity

Status

Endangered

Cheetahs Remaining: From about 9,000 to 12,000 in the wild; another 1,400 in zoos

Main Threats to Survival: shrinking habitat; vanishing prey; farmers, hunters, and poachers; genetic predisposition to disease

The Endangered Cheetah

The big cat stalks across the plain. She is long and lean. Her spots camouflage her body in the tall grass of the African savanna. Just ahead, a herd of gazelles grazes in the early morning sun. The cat crouches low, muscles tense, eyes riveted on a gazelle at the edge of the herd. She steals closer, closer, then springs.

The herd scatters. The gazelle bolts. It is quick, but the cat is quicker. In seconds the cat is a tawny blur shooting over the savanna, dodging and darting as she pursues her next meal.

▲ A cheetah stalking its prey across the African savanna.

The cat is a cheetah, the fastest animal on land, which can reach speeds of up to 70 miles per hour (112 kilometers per hour). Unfortunately, this endangered species is also racing toward extinction.

The Cheetah's Role in History

Cheetahs are one of the world's big cats. Scientists usually group seven species into the category of big cats: tigers, lions, leopards, jaguars, cheetahs, snow leopards, and pumas. (Pumas are North American cats that are also called cougars or mountain lions). Of all the big-cat species, cheetahs are one of the most endangered.

The slender, spotted cheetah once roamed four continents: North America, where it is thought the species originated; Europe; all of Africa; and Asia from the Middle East to India. Ancient Sumerians kept cheetahs as pets. Ancient Egyptians worshiped the cheetah as the goddess Mafdet. The Egyptians believed cheetahs carried the souls of their dead pharaohs, or rulers, into the afterlife.

Cheetahs are easier to tame than other big cats, and captive cheetahs became a status symbol for African, Asian, and European rulers. Charlemagne, the first emperor of the Holy Roman Empire; Genghis Khan, a Mongol emperor; and Kublai Khan, Genghis Khan's grandson, all kept pet cheetahs. In the 1500s, Indian emperor Akbar the Great kept thousands of cheetahs and trained them to hunt. Middle Eastern royalty used cheetahs to hunt gazelles, and European nobles used cheetahs to hunt for sport. For centuries, people called cheetahs the "hunting leopard."

As recently as 1900, about one hundred thousand cheetahs still survived throughout their traditional range. By 1960, that number had dropped to about fifty thousand.

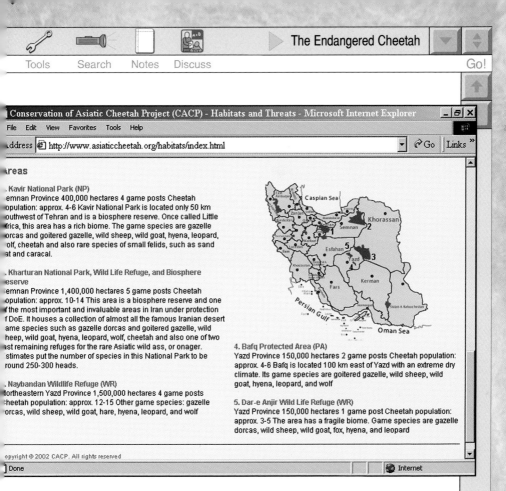

Conservation of Asiatic Cheetah Project (CACP) - Habitats and Threats - Microsoft Internet Explorer   _ 🗗 ✕

File   Edit   View   Favorites   Tools   Help

Address 📄 http://www.asiaticcheetah.org/habitats/index.html   ▼   🖑 Go   Links »

reas

. Kavir National Park (NP)
emnan Province 400,000 hectares 4 game posts Cheetah
opulation: approx. 4-6 Kavir National Park is located only 50 km
outhwest of Tehran and is a biosphere reserve. Once called Little
frica, this area has a rich biome. The game species are gazelle
orcas and goitered gazelle, wild sheep, wild goat, hyena, leopard,
olf, cheetah and also rare species of small felids, such as sand
at and caracal.

. Kharturan National Park, Wild Life Refuge, and Biosphere
eserve
emnan Province 1,400,000 hectares 5 game posts Cheetah
opulation: approx. 10-14 This area is a biosphere reserve and one
f the most important and invaluable areas in Iran under protection
f DoE. It houses a collection of almost all the famous Iranian desert
ame species such as gazelle dorcas and goitered gazelle, wild
heep, wild goat, hyena, leopard, wolf, cheetah and also one of two
ast remaining refuges for the rare Asiatic wild ass, or onager. It
stimates put the number of species in this National Park to be
round 250-300 heads.

. Naybandan Wildlife Refuge (WR)
lortheastern Yazd Province 1,500,000 hectares 4 game posts
:heetah population: approx. 12-15 Other game species: gazelle
orcas, wild sheep, wild goat, hare, hyena, leopard, and wolf

4. Bafq Protected Area (PA)
Yazd Province 150,000 hectares 2 game posts Cheetah population:
approx. 4-6 Bafq is located 100 km east of Yazd with an extreme dry
climate. Its game species are goitered gazelle, wild sheep, wild
goat, hyena, leopard, and wolf

5. Dar-e Anjir Wild Life Refuge (WR)
Yazd Province 150,000 hectares 1 game post Cheetah population:
approx. 3-5 The area has a fragile biome. Game species are gazelle
dorcas, wild sheep, wild goat, fox, hyena, and leopard

Done   🌐 Internet

⚠ Most of the cheetahs left in Asia live in Iran. The Conservation of
Asiatic Cheetah Project is trying to save the few hundred cheetahs
that remain in this Middle Eastern country.

Today, only between 9,000 and 12,000 cheetahs remain in
the wild, and that number continues to decline. Cheetahs
have been squeezed out of the largest part of their former
territory, and most of today's cheetahs exist in the grassy
plains and woodlands of central and southern Africa. The
largest population of wild cheetahs lives in the southern
African country of Namibia. A handful of Asian cheetahs—
fewer than two hundred—live in a remote mountain region
in northwestern Iran. About 1,400 cheetahs live in captivity in zoos and other facilities around the world.[1]

▷ Vanishing Territory

Other animals pose a threat to the cheetah's survival. Predators such as lions, leopards, and hyenas will steal a cheetah's food and will kill cheetah cubs and sometimes kill adult cheetahs. But these predators are not the cheetah's worst enemy. The cheetah's most dangerous enemy, by far, is man. It is not a coincidence that in the last hundred years, as the human population has exploded, the cheetah population has plummeted.

One of the biggest problems that cheetahs face is shrinking habitat. Cheetahs need lots of space. They are solitary animals that roam vast areas of land, hunting prey. As the human population has increased, more and more people have moved into the cheetah's traditional territory. People clear land to build houses, cities, and highways. Farmers plow land for crops and fence it off to graze farm animals such as sheep and cattle. Humans have destroyed much of the cheetah's natural habitat and have broken the remaining habitat into smaller patches.

As we crowd cheetahs into smaller areas, we also force them into closer quarters with other predators, such as lions, leopards, and hyenas. Cheetahs are excellent hunters, but they are not powerful fighters. They cannot protect themselves, their cubs, or their killed prey from these larger, stronger predators.

▷ Disappearing Prey

When humans clear the cheetah's habitat for farmland, they push out the cheetah's natural prey: gazelles, impalas, and other medium-sized ungulates, or hoofed animals. In the early twentieth century, hunters wiped out the gazelle population in the Arab peninsula. With no prey to hunt, cheetahs soon disappeared from the region. In the 1920s, cheetahs vanished from Iraq. In 1959, the last cheetah in Israel was spotted. In 1962, the last cheetahs in Jordan, a female and her cub, were shot, and in 1977, the last cheetah in Oman was killed.

In India, the cheetah's favorite prey was an antelope called the black buck. In the late 1800s and early 1900s, hunters killed black bucks by the thousands. At the same time, India's population swelled, and farmers forced the black buck from its natural habitat. The black buck's population dropped to only a few thousand. As the cheetah's prey disappeared, the cheetah, too, vanished. By 1952, the cheetah was extinct in India.

▲ The Thomson's gazelle has long been natural prey for cheetahs. But as more and more gazelles are driven from their habitat, cheetahs must turn elsewhere for food.

15

▷ Farmers, Hunters, and Poachers

Many African farmers are not concerned that cheetahs are endangered. In fact, many farmers wish the cheetah would become extinct. They do not see cheetahs as sleek, beautiful, endangered animals but as dangerous pests that threaten their livestock and their livelihood—much the way many American farmers view coyotes.

When farmers take over land for farming, they not only take the cheetah's habitat, but they also take the habitat of the cheetah's natural prey. If cheetahs cannot find wild animals for food, they will kill farm animals such as sheep, goats, and calves. Lions and leopards also kill farm animals, but these predators hunt at night. Cheetahs hunt during the day. They are the predators that farmers see, so they are the predators that farmers blame. Every year, African farmers and ranchers shoot or trap hundreds of cheetahs to protect their livestock.

Farmers are not the only humans who kill cheetahs. The cheetah is a protected species, but many African countries still allow hunters to kill or capture a small number of cheetahs each year. Illegal hunters, called poachers, do not bother with hunting permits. Poachers hunt cheetahs even in protected wildlife preserves.

Some poachers and hunters kill for the cheetah's spotted fur. Some kill cheetahs as a trophy sport. They like the challenge of tracking down and killing the fastest animal on land. Other hunters and poachers capture cheetah cubs to be sold as pets. To catch the cubs, they often kill the mother cheetah. Hunters and poachers also kill gazelles, antelopes, and other cheetah prey. When their natural food sources are killed off, cheetahs face starvation—and more conflict with farmers.

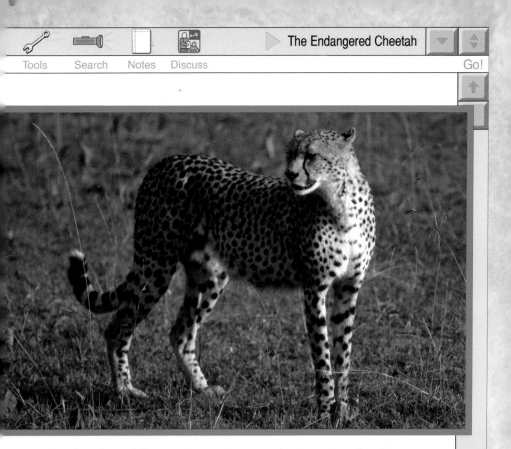

▲ *Their beautiful spotted coats have made cheetahs vulnerable to hunters and poachers.*

▷ More Problems

People and organizations around the world are working to save cheetahs from extinction. But cheetahs have several problems that make the species difficult to protect. For example, about 90 percent of all wild cheetah cubs die before they reach adulthood.[2] Most of these cheetah cubs are killed by large predators, especially lions. This problem becomes worse when cheetahs and lions are forced to share smaller territories. Wildlife preserves protect many endangered animals. But cheetahs do not fare well in preserves, where they must compete with lions, hyenas, and other large predators for prey and living space.

Cheetahs are also very similar to one another genetically. Scientists have found that all cheetahs are as closely related as twins. This genetic similarity makes the cheetah population vulnerable to disease and less able to adapt to changes in their environment. Scientists suspect genetic similarity is one of the reasons that cheetahs do not breed well in captivity.

Other big cats, such as tigers, lions, leopards, and pumas, sometimes attack and kill humans. But a cheetah has never been known to attack a human without being provoked. Cheetahs face much more danger from us than we have ever faced from the cheetah. And now it is up to us to ensure that these fast, sleek cats continue to survive.

▲ *The remarkable genetic similarities between all cheetahs makes them less able to resist disease, adapt to changes in their environment, and breed in captivity.*

Chapter 2 ▶

The Fastest Animal on Land

The cheetah is so different from other big cats that it is the only animal in its genus, *Acinonyx*. Its full scientific name is *Acinonyx jubatus*. Its common name, *cheetah*, comes from the Sanskrit word *citrakaya*, which means "speckled body."

Cheetahs are one of the oldest cats. They evolved from the first catlike mammal about 5 million years ago, over 3 million years before lions, tigers, leopards, and jaguars appeared. Scientists believe cheetahs originated in what is today Texas, Nevada, and Wyoming. At least four ancient cheetah species once roamed over North America, Europe, Africa, and Asia. One giant cheetah species was twice as big as today's cheetah or about the size of the modern lion. These other cheetah species died out between ten thousand and twenty thousand years ago. Only *Acinonyx jubatus* remains.

▶ A Spotted Cat

Cheetahs have tawny (golden tan) fur with black spots that cover their bodies except their throats and stomachs, which are white. Black lines called "tear marks" run from the inner corners of their eyes to the corners of their mouth. Scientists believe these tear marks help protect cheetahs' eyes from the glare of the sun when they hunt, the same way that black grease under football and baseball players' eyes deflects the sun's glare during games. Tear

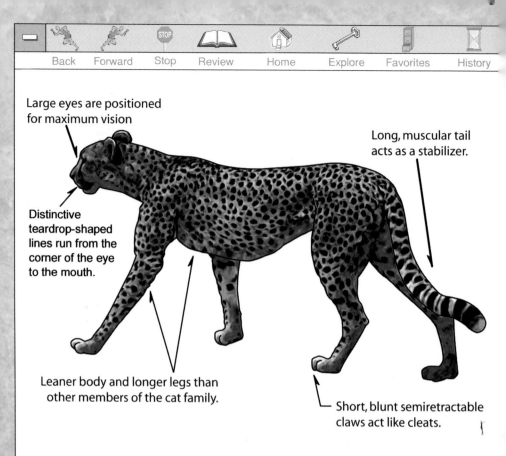

Large eyes are positioned for maximum vision

Long, muscular tail acts as a stabilizer.

Distinctive teardrop-shaped lines run from the corner of the eye to the mouth.

Leaner body and longer legs than other members of the cat family.

Short, blunt semiretractable claws act like cleats.

▲ *Cheetahs, the fastest land animals, are built for speed.*

marks make it easy to distinguish cheetahs from other spotted cats, such as leopards and jaguars.

Full-grown cheetahs weigh 80 to 140 pounds (36 to 64 kilograms). Their bodies average 4 ½ feet (1 ½ meters) in length, and their tails add another 30 inches (76 centimeters). Males are slightly larger than females, and Asian cheetahs are larger and have darker coloring than African cheetahs. Asian cheetahs also have longer fur.

People sometimes confuse cheetahs with leopards and jaguars since all three cats are similar in size and coloring and all have spots. But cheetahs' spots are solid black, while leopards and jaguars have solid spots on their legs and heads but rosette spots—black spots with tawny centers—across their bodies. The jaguar's rosettes have small black spots in the middle. Cheetahs are also lankier than leopards and jaguars. They have smaller heads, longer legs, and are not as heavy. Leopards and jaguars do not have tear marks. Leopards live throughout Africa and Asia, and their territory overlaps the cheetah's. Jaguars live in Central America and South America.

The King of Cheetahs

In 1926, Major A. L. Cooper spotted an unusual cheetah in southern Africa, in what is now the country of Zimbabwe. Instead of the usual small spots, this cheetah had elongated, irregular splotches across its body and three long stripes down its back. It looked so different from other cheetahs that scientists thought it must be a separate subspecies. They gave it the name *Acinonyx rex*, or king cheetah. They wondered if it could be a crossbreed between a cheetah and a leopard. Over the next five decades, only a handful of king cheetahs were spotted in the wild. No king cheetahs existed in captivity.

But in 1981, a female cheetah at the De Wildt Cheetah and Wildlife Centre in South Africa gave birth to a king cheetah cub. The cub's parents, as well as the four other cubs in the litter, had normal spotted markings. Researchers realized that the king cheetah was not a separate subspecies. Aside from the unusual markings on its coat, the king cheetah was just like all other cheetahs. Its stripes were simply a rare genetic variation.

Built for Speed

Over short distances, cheetahs are the fastest animals on earth. They can go from a dead stop to 60 miles per hour (96 kilometers per hour) in three seconds.[1] They can

sprint up to 70 miles an hour (112 kilometers an hour) for up to 600 yards (550 meters). They streak along in strides of 22 feet (6.7 meters), which is longer than an average pickup truck. These short sprints are exhausting and last less than a minute.

Every part of the cheetah's long, streamlined body is adapted to help it run fast. A cheetah has light bones and a long, flexible spine that coils in and then springs out into a stretch as the cheetah runs. Its hind legs come so far forward with each stride that its hind paws are actually in front of its front legs. All four paws leave the ground when the cheetah flexes forward and again when it stretches into its stride, so that during a chase the cheetah is airborne over 50 percent of the time. The cheetah's vertical shoulder blades are not attached to its small collarbone, which allows its shoulders to move more freely and helps lengthen its stride. Its small, light head gives the cheetah less wind resistance, and its long flattened tail acts as a rudder, helping the cheetah keep its balance and navigate quick, sharp turns as it chases its prey.

A cheetah's large eyes are set high on its head to give it maximum binocular vision, or vision through two eyes. Binocular vision allows the cheetah to see the world as three-dimensional, helping it judge depth and distance. Its eyes have an elongated fovea—the depression in the center of the retina—that gives it extraordinarily keen vision in bright light. This is important because cheetahs usually hunt during the day, under the bright sun of the African savanna. A membrane covers the cheetah's eyes to protect them from flying dust that is kicked up during a chase.

Cheetahs have long, lean legs. Tissue binds the bones of their lower hind legs together, which gives the cheetah

Tools   Search   Notes   Discuss   Go!

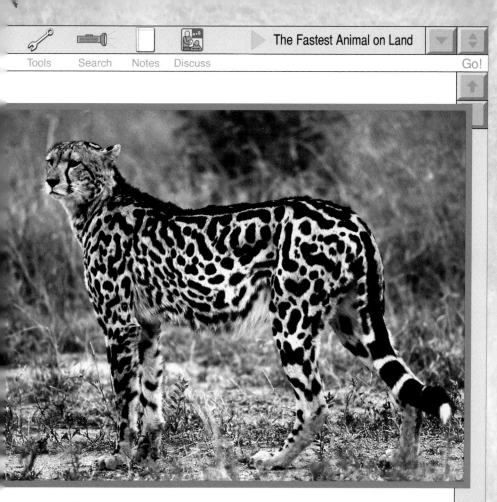

▲ *This rare king cheetah is marked by its irregular and elongated spots and dark stripes running along its spine.*

sure footing and protects its legs from the impact during a chase. All cats can retract their claws, or draw them back into their paws. But cheetahs lack the sheath of skin that hides and protects other cats' claws, so a cheetah's claws are always visible. These semiretractable claws dig into the earth like cleats, and the cheetah's hard foot pads are ridged, similar to tire treads, giving them traction for running and sharp cornering.

Such high-speed sprints require lots of oxygen. The cheetah's internal organs have adapted to supply oxygen

This cheetah's large eyes, set high on its head, give it the keen vision it needs to spy its prey at a distance.

and release carbon dioxide quickly and efficiently. Its enlarged nostrils, sinus cavities, and lungs pull in large amounts of oxygen. Its oversized heart and muscular arteries pump the oxygen rapidly through its body. Cheetahs also have large livers that are able to convert stored energy to the fuel their bodies need for the chase.

Cat or Dog?

Cheetahs are so different from other cats that throughout history, many people believed cheetahs were members of the dog family or a mix of cat and dog. The cheetah does have characteristics that, on the surface, resemble those of a dog.

A cheetah's long, lean legs, high shoulders, and long, tufted neck give it a wolflike appearance. Its paws and claws, too, seem to belong more to a dog than to a cat. When cheetah cubs are born, their claws are as sharp as any cat's claws. But the cheetah's semiretractable claws are constantly exposed, especially during lightning-fast chases. Everyday wear and tear dulls the claws until they are more

▲ *The high-speed sprints of a cheetah as it races to catch its prey also tire the cat quickly.*

like the blunt claws of a dog than the needle-sharp claws of a cat. A cheetah's foot pads are hard and tough like a dog's instead of supple like a typical cat's. The blunt claws and hard pads help explain why, unlike most cats, cheetahs are poor tree climbers.

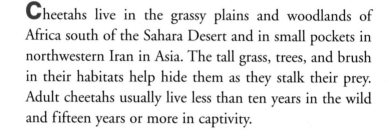

Life as a Cheetah

Cheetahs live in the grassy plains and woodlands of Africa south of the Sahara Desert and in small pockets in northwestern Iran in Asia. The tall grass, trees, and brush in their habitats help hide them as they stalk their prey. Adult cheetahs usually live less than ten years in the wild and fifteen years or more in captivity.

▷ The Cheetah's Family

Female cheetahs live alone except when they have cubs. Each female roams a home range, or area of land, that she hunts. Female ranges often overlap, but female cheetahs go to great lengths to avoid each other. A female's range can cover more than 300 square miles (800 square kilometers).[1] Her range is large because she needs to find enough prey to feed herself and her cubs and find hiding places for them. A mother cheetah moves her cubs every two to three days, trying to keep them safe from predators.

Female cheetahs have litters of one to eight cubs, although three to five is average. Cubs weigh less than 10 ounces (300 grams) at birth. They have gray coats and dark bellies. A light-colored spiky mantle, or tuft of long fur, covers their heads, shoulders, and backs. The mantle may protect the cubs in two ways: It makes them resemble the more aggressive honey badger, an animal that predators usually avoid, and it helps the cubs blend into tall grass.

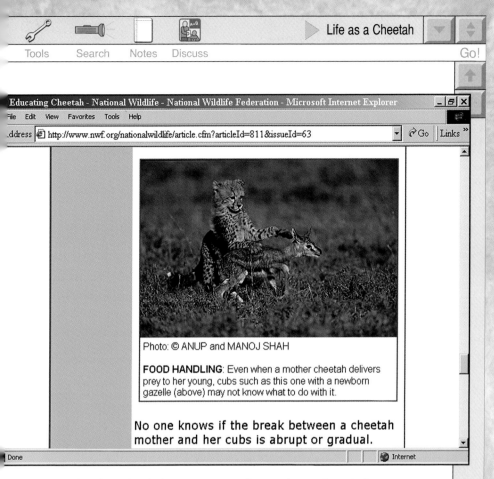

Photo: © ANUP and MANOJ SHAH

FOOD HANDLING: Even when a mother cheetah delivers prey to her young, cubs such as this one with a newborn gazelle (above) may not know what to do with it.

No one knows if the break between a cheetah mother and her cubs is abrupt or gradual.

▲ This cheetah cub does not seem to know what to do with the young gazelle that the cub's mother has brought to it.

When cheetah cubs are about eighteen months old, their mother leaves them to breed. The nearly grown cubs stay together for about six more months. The females then set off on their own. The males either stay together or strike out on their own as solitary males.

Male cheetahs do not help females raise cubs. Males sometimes live alone, but often they live in coalitions, or groups, of two or three. The males in these coalitions are usually brothers from the same litter. Male ranges are much smaller than female ranges—about 20 square miles (58 square kilometers).[2] Males mark their hunting ranges by spraying urine and fiercely defend their territory from other male cheetahs.

The Cheetah's Chirp

Lions, tigers, leopards, and jaguars—sometimes called the great cats—let out deep, bone-rattling roars that can be heard for over a mile. But cheetahs lack the stretchy ligaments in their throats that allow the great cats to roar. Instead, cheetahs growl, hiss, and yelp to ward off intruders. They purr just like a house cat when they are content. The female coos like a dove when she is ready to mate. Perhaps the most unexpected sound to come from the

▲ A herd of wildebeest graze on the Serengeti, a vast plains area of northern Tanzania that is also a national park. There are more than 2 million wildebeest in Serengeti National Park, which helps to provide the park's cheetahs with some of the prey they need to survive.

cheetah is its chirp. When cheetah mothers and their cubs call to each other, they sound more like birds than cats.

▷ The Hunt

Cheetahs are carnivores, or meat eaters. They prey on a variety of species from rabbits and small antelopes, such as the Thomson's gazelle, to the young of larger antelope, such as wildebeest. These are all very fast animals. In fact, the speed of a gazelle is second only to that of a cheetah.

Cheetahs are efficient hunters. They successfully bring down their prey in about half their hunts. This is especially impressive when compared to the success rates of other predators. Lions, for example, are powerful hunters, but they succeed in capturing their prey in less than one fifth of their hunts.[3] Cheetahs must be efficient. They can sprint at 60 to 70 miles per hour (97 to 112 kilometers per hour) but can only keep up that pace for less than a minute. So cheetahs cannot rely on speed alone to catch their food. They must also be clever and patient.

Cheetahs hunt mostly during the day, usually in the cool of the early morning or late afternoon. Their keen vision and sense of smell help them to hunt. They often climb onto a tall termite mound or the low branch of a tree to get a better long-distance view. Once a cheetah spots a herd of gazelle or antelope, it stalks the animals, creeping through the grass or brush until it is within a hundred feet of its prey. The cheetah is faster than the gazelle or antelope, but it cannot run great distances, so the cheetah must get as close as possible. If its prey gets too much of a head start, the cheetah cannot catch it. When the prey is within striking distance, the cheetah bursts into high gear and gives chase, staying on the animal's tail as it dodges and turns. Finally, the cheetah

overtakes the prey and trips the animal with its front foot, using a claw called the dewclaw, which is on the inside of its foreleg, to snag the prey's leg.

Once the animal is brought down, the cheetah clamps its jaws around the prey's throat. But rather than biting a gazelle or antelope to kill it, the cheetah closes off the animal's air pipe and suffocates it. Suffocation can take up to twenty minutes, which is about the same amount of time the cheetah needs to recover from the exhausting hunt. The cheetah's large nostrils and nasal passages help the cheetah catch its breath as it clamps down on the prey's throat.

During the chase, a cheetah's body temperature can reach 105°F (40.6°C). Its heart rate increases from a

▲ *A cheetah springs into action as it begins its attack. When a cheetah spots prey, it needs to get as close as possible to its target since it cannot run for long.*

resting rate of 120 to 170 beats per minute to 200 to 250 beats per minute, and its breathing can increase to more than 150 breaths per minute from its resting rate of about 16 breaths per minute.[4]

▷ The Trade-off

The adaptations that give cheetahs blinding speed also make them poor fighters. The slender cheetah is no match for the much stronger and more muscular lion or leopard. The cheetah's relatively weak jaws and blunted claws are not effective weapons, and its teeth are not as large as those of other cats. The cheetah's head is small, and its enlarged nasal passages take up a large amount of space, leaving less room for teeth.

Because it cannot defend itself by fighting, the cheetah does its best to avoid other predators, which may be another reason that the cheetah, unlike most big cats, hunts by day. The hunt also saps a cheetah's strength, so when another predator—a lion, leopard, hyena, jackal, or wild dog—tries to steal the cheetah's kill, the exhausted cheetah will not fight back. It will simply walk away. Even a flock of vultures can drive a cheetah from its kill. Vultures attract lions and other large predators, who know that vultures gather over dead animals. It is much easier for the cheetah to catch another gazelle than to fight a stronger animal and risk injury, since an injured cheetah could face starvation.

Cheetahs hunt every one to three days and eat as much as they can immediately after the kill. Then they abandon their prey, rather than saving and hiding it as leopards do. Cheetahs rarely scavenge, or eat animals that are already dead. Saved prey and scavenged prey attract other predators, which cheetahs need to avoid.

Threats to Cheetahs

Cheetahs face the same major problems that most endangered species face: loss of habitat, loss of prey, and slaughter at the hands of humans who do not know or care that their species is nearing extinction. But cheetahs are unique cats facing a unique problem: their lack of genetic diversity.

▷ A Genetic Bottleneck

In 1981, a team of scientists led by Dr. Stephen J. O'Brien began studying the genes of cheetahs. Genes are the material in cells that carry the information that living things inherit from their parents. Genes determine the traits an animal will possess, such as size, length of legs, and fur color and pattern. When Dr. O'Brien and his team analyzed cheetah genes, they found something startling: The genes of all cheetahs are nearly identical. In most animal species, the individual members of a family share about 80 percent of the same genes, but in cheetahs, that figure climbs to about 99 percent.[1]

Dr. O'Brien's team concluded that cheetahs came very close to extinction ten thousand to twelve thousand years ago, at the end of the last ice age, and that only a handful of cheetahs survived. That number could have been as low as one pregnant female cheetah. With no unrelated pairs to breed, cheetahs would have had to breed with close family members, in what is called inbreeding. If the conclusion reached by Dr. O'Brien and his team is correct, it means that all cheetahs today descend from those few survivors and their small gene pool.

Cheetahs in Captivity

Zoos and research facilities can often help save endangered species through breeding programs. Captive-bred animals can replace older zoo animals that die so that zoos do not need to take more animals from the wild. Zoos can also breed some species for release back into their natural habitat, increasing the number of animals in the wild. And zoos are sometimes the last refuge for an endangered

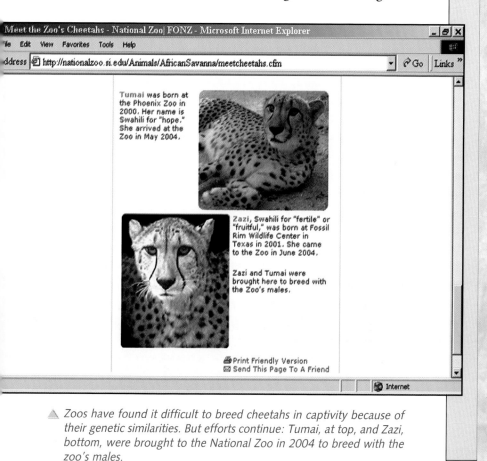

Meet the Zoo's Cheetahs - National Zoo| FONZ - Microsoft Internet Explorer

File Edit View Favorites Tools Help

Address http://nationalzoo.si.edu/Animals/AfricanSavanna/meetcheetahs.cfm   Go   Links

Tumai was born at the Phoenix Zoo in 2000. Her name is Swahili for "hope." She arrived at the Zoo in May 2004.

Zazi, Swahili for "fertile" or "fruitful," was born at Fossil Rim Wildlife Center in Texas in 2001. She came to the Zoo in June 2004.

Zazi and Tumai were brought here to breed with the Zoo's males.

Print Friendly Version
Send This Page To A Friend

Internet

▲ Zoos have found it difficult to breed cheetahs in captivity because of their genetic similarities. But efforts continue: Tumai, at top, and Zazi, bottom, were brought to the National Zoo in 2004 to breed with the zoo's males.

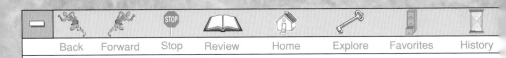
species. For example, Przewalski's horse, a wild central Asian horse, now exists only in captivity. Przewalski's horse is extinct in the wild.

But zoos have found it difficult to help the cheetah because cheetahs do not breed well in captivity. In the 1500s, Indian emperor Akbar the Great kept about nine thousand cheetahs during his forty-nine-year reign. In that time, his cheetahs were only able to produce one litter of cubs. That litter was the only known litter born in captivity until 1956, when a female cheetah gave birth at the Philadelphia Zoo, but those cubs lived only three months. Since 1956, only 17 percent of captive cheetahs have successfully given birth, and of those cubs born, 30 to 40 percent have died at a young age.

Scientists believe genetic similarity is one of the reasons that cheetahs do not breed well in captivity. Inbreeding can cause birth defects. It can also make an animal infertile, or unable to breed. Scientists have found that many male cheetahs have low levels of sperm, or reproductive cells. Up to 70 percent of their sperm is genetically weak or abnormal.

Disease

Inbreeding also leaves a species vulnerable to disease. Dr. O'Brien and his team tested the genetic similarity of the cheetah's immune system by using skin grafts. In a genetically diverse species, skin can only be successfully transplanted between close relatives, such as brothers and sisters or parents and children. The body will reject a skin graft from an unrelated individual. The immune system will identify the skin graft as foreign material and try to get rid of it. But skin grafts between unrelated cheetahs were not rejected—the grafts healed perfectly. The cheetahs'

http://wcs.org/media/file/Cashewsitting640.jpg - Microsoft Internet Explorer

File   Edit   View   Favorites   Tools   Help

ddress http://wcs.org/media/file/Cashewsitting640.jpg   Go Links

Done   Internet

▲ *Scientists from the Wildlife Conservation Society and the Zoological Society of London have been tracking individual cheetahs in the Serengeti National Park (and giving them interesting names) for twenty years. This cheetah, Cashew, born in 1998, has not been seen since 2002, however, and scientists fear she may no longer be alive.*

genes were so similar that their immune systems did not recognize the transplanted skin as foreign matter.

When a species has genetic diversity, some animals in that species will be more likely to develop disease. Other animals in the species will possess genes in their immune system that will resist disease. But in a species that is genetically similar, a disease that affects one animal will likely affect all the animals. A single disease could wipe out the entire species.

An example is feline infectious peritonitis, or FIP, which is caused by a virus. Less than 5 percent of house cats that come down with FIP die from it. But in the 1980s, FIP struck Wildlife Safari, a wildlife conservation park and research facility in Oregon. Sixty percent of the park's cheetahs and 85 percent of the cheetah cubs died.[2] Their genetic similarity made the park's cheetah population more vulnerable to the disease. The park has had many successes, however, breeding cheetahs. There have been 133 cubs born at Wildlife Safari since 1973, and in May 2004, Wildlife Safari welcomed the birth of four cubs, two males and two females, the first cheetah cubs to be born there in five years.[3]

The Good News

The good news is that the cheetah's genetic similarity has not kept it from reproducing in the wild. When a cheetah mother loses her cubs, she breeds again almost immediately.

Ninety to ninety-five percent of wild cheetah cubs die when they are very young. But research shows that lions, hyenas, and other predators kill most of the cubs. Only a small number die from birth defects or other problems associated with inbreeding.

Wild cheetahs are also less vulnerable than captive cheetahs to disease epidemics. Cheetahs are partly solitary. Females live with their own cubs, and males live alone or in a coalition with one or two other males. Since they avoid contact with other cheetahs, disease does not spread rapidly through the wild cheetah population.

Chapter 5 ▶

Saving the Cheetah

The worldwide cheetah population continues to decline. If cheetahs are to survive, biologists, zookeepers, and other cheetah specialists need to learn all they can about cheetahs and their behavior. They also need to find ways to accommodate the cheetah's unique traits as they work to save the species.

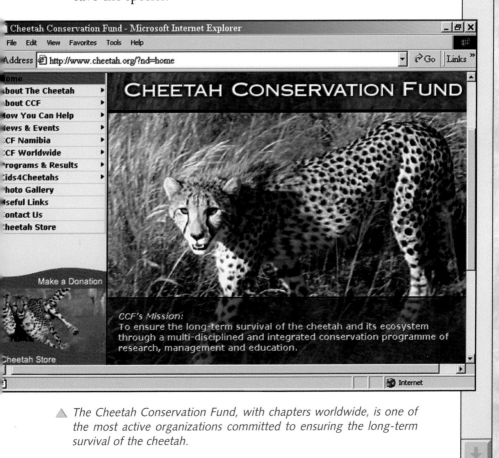

△ The Cheetah Conservation Fund, with chapters worldwide, is one of the most active organizations committed to ensuring the long-term survival of the cheetah.

▷ Breeding in Captivity

Zoos are using what they have learned about wild cheetah behavior to help cheetahs breed in captivity. Traditionally, zoos have exhibited male and female cheetahs together in relatively small spaces. For many animal species, keeping pairs of males and females together is effective, and the animal pairs produce offspring.

But over the past twenty years, zoos have begun creating exhibit spaces that allow captive cheetahs to live more like wild cheetahs, since they have found that female cheetahs do not breed when they are constantly with a male. And rather than keeping them confined, zoos give cheetahs open spaces to wander. The cheetahs obviously cannot prey on a zoo's captive gazelle population, but zoos have tried to give cheetahs more opportunities to use their hunting instincts. They allow cheetahs to chase rags tied to a line, similar to the way greyhounds chase a mechanical rabbit around a dog track. Zoos have found that cheetahs like to be kept near gazelles, where they can watch them—even if they cannot hunt them.

In addition to keeping male and female cheetahs apart until it is time to breed, some zoos allow the female to choose her mate from a group of several males. Since all cheetahs are so similar genetically, zoos try to breed pairs of cheetahs that are as genetically different as possible. Zoos often share breeding animals, shipping a male cheetah from one zoo to be a mate for a female cheetah in another zoo. Dr. Laurie Marker, a conservation biologist who founded the Cheetah Conservation Fund (CCF), maintains the International Cheetah Studbook. This book is a record of the family trees of captive cheetahs throughout the world and is used by zoos to determine which pairs of cheetahs should breed.

▷ People Helping Cats

To save the cheetah, conservationists are also trying to educate the people who live among cheetahs. They hope to convince them that it is possible to live peacefully with earth's fastest land animal. In 1991, Dr. Laurie Marker established the CCF in Namibia with that goal in mind: to persuade Namibian farmers to stop killing the cheetahs on their land.

Namibia is home to the world's largest population of wild cheetahs. About 2,500 of the big cats live in this country in southwestern Africa. Namibia has game

▲ Dr. Laurie Marker, who helped to found the Cheetah Conservation Fund and is now its executive director, has made it one of her missions to help cheetahs and farmers in Namibia coexist peacefully.

reserves to protect its wildlife, but only about 5 percent of the country's cheetahs live in those protected areas. Since game reserves are home to the cheetah's natural enemies— lions, leopards, and hyenas—it is difficult for cheetahs to survive there. Most of Namibia's cheetahs live on the large farms outside the reserves, where lions and other large predators are less plentiful.

But on the farms, cheetahs run into another dangerous enemy: humans. Cheetahs are a protected species in Namibia, but the law allows farmers to shoot or trap "problem" animals, or animals that kill their livestock. A drought during the 1980s killed off much of the cheetah's natural prey, and the cats began killing more sheep, goats, and calves. By the time Dr. Marker arrived, farmers were killing six hundred cheetahs per year.[1]

Marker set up the CCF on three large farms and began visiting farmers across Namibia. She brought a rescued cheetah with her so that farmers could see up close what a gentle animal it was. She wanted to have the farmers understand that cheetahs killed their livestock only when their natural prey was not available. She tried to convince farmers that if they allowed gazelles and other antelope onto their lands, cheetahs would become less of a problem.

Dr. Marker put radio collars on several wild cheetahs to track their movements. In doing this, she was able to show farmers that cheetahs roam vast distances each day, proving that the cheetahs were miles away when a farm animal was killed.

Dr. Marker has succeeded in convincing many farmers to trap cheetahs rather than kill them. The farmers then call the CCF to pick up the cheetah and release it in an area where it will be less of a problem.

Dogs Helping Cats

Wildlife experts know that cheetahs are not aggressive animals—that when challenged, cheetahs would rather run than fight. Dr. Marker is using this knowledge of cheetah behavior to help Namibian farmers protect their livestock without harming cheetahs.

Marker has shown farmers that cheetahs will not harm closely guarded farm animals. Full-grown cattle are too large for cheetahs to attack, but cheetahs will hunt calves. The CCF encourages farmers to keep calves penned up close to their human herders and to raise cattle breeds that

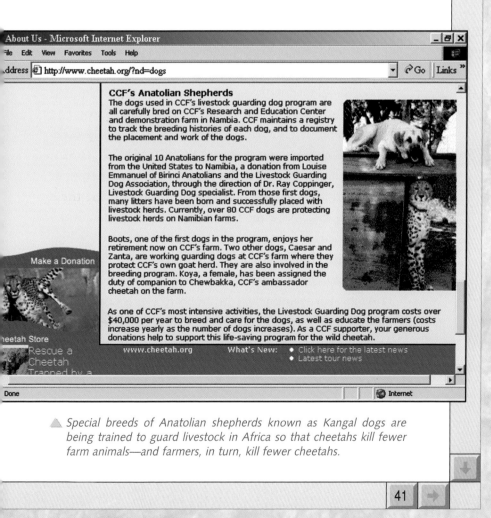

CCF's Anatolian Shepherds

The dogs used in CCF's livestock guarding dog program are all carefully bred on CCF's Research and Education Center and demonstration farm in Namibia. CCF maintains a registry to track the breeding histories of each dog, and to document the placement and work of the dogs.

The original 10 Anatolians for the program were imported from the United States to Namibia, a donation from Louise Emmanuel of Birinci Anatolians and the Livestock Guarding Dog Association, through the direction of Dr. Ray Coppinger, Livestock Guarding Dog specialist. From those first dogs, many litters have been born and successfully placed with livestock herds. Currently, over 80 CCF dogs are protecting livestock herds on Namibian farms.

Boots, one of the first dogs in the program, enjoys her retirement now on CCF's farm. Two other dogs, Caesar and Zanta, are working guarding dogs at CCF's farm where they protect CCF's own goat herd. They are also involved in the breeding program. Koya, a female, has been assigned the duty of companion to Chewbakka, CCF's ambassador cheetah on the farm.

As one of CCF's most intensive activities, the Livestock Guarding Dog program costs over $40,000 per year to breed and care for the dogs, as well as educate the farmers (costs increase yearly as the number of dogs increases). As a CCF supporter, your generous donations help to support this life-saving program for the wild cheetah.

▲ Special breeds of Anatolian shepherds known as Kangal dogs are being trained to guard livestock in Africa so that cheetahs kill fewer farm animals—and farmers, in turn, kill fewer cheetahs.

strongly protect their young. The CCF also recommends that farmers keep a few donkeys with their herds of cattle, sheep, and goats. Donkeys are aggressive and will drive away predators such as cheetahs and jackals.

In the past few years, the CCF has also begun training a special breed of Anatolian shepherd known as a Kangal dog to guard Namibian livestock. The dogs watch over the farm animals and bark at intruders. Timid cheetahs and even bolder predators such as leopards run from the barking dogs. Since 1994, the CCF has given more than two hundred Kangal dogs to Namibian farmers.

Kill Them to Save Them?

Surprisingly, some conservationists think trophy hunters could help save the cheetah. They believe African governments should allow big-game hunters to kill a limited number of cheetahs on private ranches and farms. The governments would require each hunter to pay a hefty fee—several thousand dollars—for the right to hunt a cheetah. Some of that money would help pay for cheetah conservation programs. But a large part of the hunting fee would go directly to the farmer who owned the land the hunter used. If farmers could make money allowing big-game hunters to hunt cheetahs on their land, they would come to see cheetahs as valuable animals. Instead of killing cheetahs, they would be more likely to protect the cats.

Governments Helping Cats

When governments, organizations, and concerned individuals work together, they can save species from extinction. In the 1800s, farmers and hunters slaughtered Africa's southern white rhino to near extinction. By 1900, only about twenty of the rhinos remained. Conservationists and researchers began working to save the rhino, and now, a little more than one hundred years later, the southern white rhino is the most abundant rhino in the world. About eleven thousand southern white rhinos live in the wild, mostly in South Africa.[2]

Within the past thirty years, many countries have passed laws to protect cheetahs. These countries and international organizations have placed cheetahs on their endangered species lists. For example, since 1970 the United States has listed cheetahs as endangered. One hundred sixty-four countries, including most of the countries where cheetahs now live, have signed the Convention on International Trade in Endangered Species of Wild Fauna and Flora (CITES), which bans international trade of endangered plants and animals. Countries that sign the agreement agree to follow the CITES regulations. Since 1975, CITES has placed cheetahs in Appendix 1, its list of the most endangered species.

Cheetahs will only continue ▷ to survive on this planet with the help of governments, conservation organizations, and concerned individuals.

▷ The Future

Despite these protections and the work of conservationists and others, the outlook for the cheetah is mixed. Education efforts in Africa are paying off as African farmers and ranchers are beginning to understand the threat to cheetahs and are using methods to protect their livestock without harming cheetahs. Some ranchers have turned their lands into wildlife preserves to attract tourists. But Namibian wildlife officials report that farmers in Namibia still kill about 180 cheetahs each year, and many more cheetah killings go unreported.[3]

Zoos have been able to breed a small number of cheetahs in captivity. One conservation facility, the De Wildt Cheetah and Wildlife Centre in South Africa, has had remarkable success with its breeding program. Since 1971, over six hundred cheetah cubs have been born at the De Wildt Centre, including forty-four rare king cheetah cubs.[4]

Many groups, including the CCF and De Wildt Centre, as well as AfriCat in Namibia and the Serengeti Cheetah Research Project in Tanzania, are working to help the cheetah. As long as dedicated people are determined to save the cheetah from extinction, this amazing animal will continue to streak across the savanna in a tawny blur. The fastest animal on land deserves a chance to survive.

The Endangered and Threatened Wildlife List

This series is based on the Endangered and Threatened Wildlife list compiled by the U.S. Fish and Wildlife Service (USFWS). Each book explores an endangered or threatened animal, tells why it has become endangered or threatened, and explains the efforts being made to restore the species' population.

The United States Fish and Wildlife Service, in the Department of the Interior, and the National Marine Fisheries Service, in the Department of Commerce, share responsibility for administration of the Endangered Species Act.

In 1973, Congress took the farsighted step of creating the Endangered Species Act, widely regarded as the world's strongest and most effective wildlife conservation law. It set an ambitious goal: to reverse the alarming trend of human-caused extinction that threatened the ecosystems we all share.

The complete list of Endangered and Threatened Wildlife and Plants can be found at **http://endangered.fws.gov/wildlife.html#Species**.

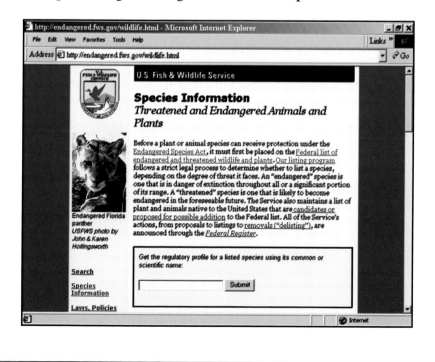

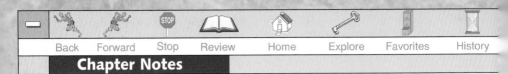
Chapter 1. The Endangered Cheetah
1. The AfriCat Foundation, "Cheetah," n.d., <http://www.africat .org/cheetah.htm> (July 1, 2004).
2. "General Information About the Cheetah," Cheetah Conservation Fund, 2004, n.d., <http://www.cheetah.org/?nd=aboutcheetah-04> (April 18, 2004).

Chapter 2. The Fastest Animal on Land
1. Paul Raffaele, "The Cheetah Runs for Its Life," *Reader's Digest*, September 1999, p. 70.

Chapter 3. Life as a Cheetah
1. Richard Conniff, "Cheetahs, Ghosts of the Grasslands," *National Geographic*, December 1999, p. 15.
2. Ibid.
3. Stephen J. O'Brien, *Tears of the Cheetah* (New York: St. Martin's Press, 2003), p. 38.
4. The De Wildt Cheetah and Wildlife Centre, "The Cheetah," n.d., <http://www.dewildt.org.za/cheetah/> (July 1, 2004).

Chapter 4. Threats to Cheetahs
1. Stephen J. O'Brien, *Tears of the Cheetah* (New York: St. Martin's Press, 2003), p. 32.
2. The Cheetah Conservation Fund, "Why Does the Cheetah Lack Genetic Diversity?" n.d., <http://www.cheetah.org/?nd=aboutcheetah-03> (July 2, 2004).
3. Wildlife Safari, Winston Oregon, "Baby Cheetahs," n.d., <http://www.wildlifesafari.org/babyCheetahs.php> (July 1, 2004).

Chapter 5. Saving the Cheetah
1. Richard Conniff, "Cheetahs, Ghosts of the Grasslands," *National Geographic*, December 1999, p. 24.
2. The International Rhino Foundation, "Rhino Information: The Southern White Rhino," n.d., <http://www.rhinos-irf.org/ rhinoinformation/whiterhino/subspecies/southern.htm> (July 7, 2004).
3. Ibid.
4. The De Wildt Cheetah and Wildlife Centre, "The Cheetah Captive Breeding Project," n.d., <http://www.dewildt.org.za/ breeding/breeding_cheetah.html> (April 18, 2004).

Aaseng, Nathan. *The Cheetah*. San Diego: Lucent Books, 2000.

Bauer, Erwin A. *The Last Big Cats: An Untamed Spirit*. Stillwater, Minn.: Voyageur Press, 2003.

Hunter, Luke. *Cheetahs*. Stillwater, Minn.: Voyageur Press, 2000.

Johansson, Philip. *The Wide Open Grasslands*. Berkeley Heights, N.J.: Enslow Publishers, Inc., 2004.

Markle, Sandra. *Outside and Inside Big Cats*. New York: Atheneum Books for Young Readers, 2002.

Saign, Geoffrey C. *The African Cats*. Danbury, Conn.: Franklin Watts, 1999.

Schlaepfer, Gloria G. *Cheetahs*. New York: Marshall Cavendish, 2002.

Thomas, Peggy. *Big Cat Conservation*. Brookfield, Conn.: Twenty-First Century Books, 2000.

Thompson, Sharon Elaine. *Built For Speed*. Minneapolis: Lerner Publications, 1998.

Weintraub, Aileen. *Discovering Africa's Land, People, and Wildlife*. Berkeley Heights, N.J.: Enslow Publishers, Inc., 2004.

A
Anatolian shepherds (Kangal dogs), 41, 42
ancient cheetahs, 12, 18
B
big cats, other species of, 12, 16, 18, 19–21, 28, 29, 31
body structure, 22–25, 29–31
breeding, 10, 18, 33, 34, 36, 38, 44
C
captivity, 10, 12, 13, 16, 18, 33–34, 36, 38
Cheetah Conservation Fund, 37, 38, 39, 40, 41, 42, 44
coloring, 10, 11, 17, 19–21, 26
cubs, 17, 21, 24, 26–27, 28, 29, 34, 36, 44
D
De Wildt Cheetah and Wildlife Centre, 21, 44
disease, 34–36
F
farmers, 14, 15, 16, 39–42, 44
fur, 10, 11, 17, 19–21, 26
G
genetic similarity, 18, 32–36
H
habitat, 10, 13, 14, 16, 26
history, 12, 19
hunters of cheetahs, 16, 42
hunting by cheetahs, 29–31
I
International Cheetah Studbook, 38

Iran, 10, 13, 26
K
king cheetahs, 21, 23, 44
M
Marker, Dr. Laurie, 38, 39–42
N
Namibia, 10, 13, 39–40, 44
O
O'Brien, Dr. Stephen J., 32–33
P
poachers, 16
predators of cheetahs, 14, 16, 17, 26, 31, 36, 40
preserves, wildlife, 17
prey, 14–15, 16, 27, 28, 29–31, 38, 40
R
ranges, 26, 27–28
S
size, 10, 20
sounds made by cheetahs, 28–29
speed, 10, 12, 21–24, 29
status, 10, 13, 14–15, 37, 43, 44
T
tear marks, 19–20
threats to survival, 14–15, 16, 17–18, 32–36, 40
W
wildlife reserves, 16, 17, 39–40, 44
Wildlife Safari (Oregon), 36